My Little Devotional Book for Busy Women

By L.S. Reed

Nashville TN

My Little Devotional Book for Busy Women / by L.S. Reed

Copyright © 2015 by Lolita S. Reed

All rights reserved. This book or any portion thereof may not be reproduced or used in any manner whatsoever without the express written permission of the publisher except for the use of brief quotations in a book review or scholarly journal.

First Printing: 2015

ISBN 978-1-943616-03-9

MAWMedia Group, LLC
2525 Somerset Drive
Nashville, TN 37217

www.mawmedia.com

Cover photo collage by Melanie J. Pullman

DEDICATION

This book is dedicated to the phenomenal women in my life, who, while they were living made my journey doable. My dear mother, Erma Mae Spight, and two sisters, Juanita Norman and Nettie Taylor, and my aunt Dorothy K. Horton. This book is also dedicated to my niece Marlene Gray, who, has been through so much, but never quits on God. I love you Marlene!

ACKNOWLEDGEMENTS

In every way and at all times, God continues to do great things for me! I owe immeasurably more praise and thanksgiving to Him for making it possible for me to complete this book than I can ever give! I thank my struggle buddy Gayle Taylor for being my go-to person and prayer covering. I thank countless friends of mine who can identify with my desire to be more like Jesus. To my sons Juan and Michael who have at times been the wind beneath my wings I love you. They are relentless in their expectations for me.

My Little Devotional Book for Busy Women

Contents

Foreword 8
Introduction 10
Week One: The Black Hole of Grief 12
Week Two: Seeking God's Comfort 15
Week Three: Angels Watching Over Me 18
Week Four: A Shelter in the Time of Trouble 21
Week Five: God the Marriage Expert 24
Week Six: The Family of God 28
Week Seven: A Victorious Life 32
Bonus Section 36
    Queen-Ship Restored: Mindset of Love Fit For a King 40
    Queen-Ship Restored: Relationship Love Fit For a King 43
    Marriage Prayer 46
About The Author 48

Foreword

In the fast pace of today, we get the feeling that things are picking up in speed. Those of us who are trying to keep up with the pace of "change" are at odds with the rapidity of progress. One former president of a local college in Denver, Colorado USA, gave an interesting observation. He said that the technology segment of society was sending so much information that by the second semester of school the college's new curriculum was outdated!

Those who make sure the latest of everything gets to the public do quite well in their job. Yet with all the hustle, we find that some things never change. One thing that stays the same is the needs females have such as attention to their physical, mental, emotional, social, and spiritual well-being. This is true of females whether that female is in the slower paced life-style of Equatorial Papua, New Guinea, or the more jet set societies of major cities like Denver, Colorado USA; Seoul, South Korea, or Nairobi, Kenya. The female spirit was intended by God, to be on a continuous maintenance plan on all levels. Thankfully, people such as Chaplain Lolita Reed are aware of this great need. She and others like her, continue to seek ways to encourage and advance women towards self-care.

In following up on Chaplain Reed's perfection of her work, I learned that she developed a series of gender- specific Bible studies. She began working on them while matriculating through Andrews University Theological Seminary located in Berrien Springs, Michigan USA. Her Bible studies created for women a quick and easy reader-friendly series called "Satin and Lace", which caters to the busy woman. These studies have evolved to become elegant gift-like cards. Chaplain Reed has what it takes to meet the busy woman's need for simplicity as well as elegance. She does this with a womanly expression of grace that feeds the spirit of women everywhere.

Womanly self-care depends a lot on how appealing or not it is to us. It depends also on our awareness, that we need balance in our lives. What Chaplain Reed's materials do is put in place simplistic and doable models. In consideration of the busy woman's need for down-time, Chaplain Reed's materials are also convenient, and time conscious.

"My Little Devotional Book for Busy Women" is one example of gender-specific materials created by Chaplain Reed for busy women. Chaplain Reed provides an easy, practical way to connect the spiritual side of women to God in much of her works. Her materials motivate women to take the time to connect with God and move on to building a relationship with Him. Her devotional materials delight the female spirit and are fast becoming a favorite of women everywhere. You will also want to acquire her poetry books for your personal library as well. Chaplain Reed's knack for keeping women on the edge of their seats and spiritually fine-tuned is truly a "kiss from God".

Gayle Taylor, Founder of "New Thing Sisters" Ministries

Introduction

These days I am a woman of leisure more or less. That does not mean I have nothing to do. In fact I have just about as much to do now as when I was working full-time plus rearing my four sons. By profession I am a Chaplain. I went to all the right schools and completed all of the requirements, but for circumstances beyond my control, I never was employed permanently as a Chaplain. Instead I did whatever work was available to provide for my family.

It's funny how women by design are always doing something. It doesn't matter what. We will find something to do if necessary. The twenty-first century woman has mastered the art of being. We will be there for whomever. But, most women fall short when it comes to self-care—generally speaking. I was guilty of that very thing until one day I realized I had nothing left to give. My health began to take a downward spin in 2002. In 2004, my son William was killed in a house fire that was set intentionally. William was twenty-nine at the time of his death. That was an incredible blow for me as a mother! In 2008, my first born son, James died from congestive heart failure. He was forty-one when he passed. I have two sons remaining (Juan and Michael) and I thank God for them every day. As much as I can be I am there for them.

Where do I find the time and where with all to be there for me? The answer is simple; I don't! I just make myself available to God, and He does the rest. Because God is the "I Am", the First, Last and all the stuff in between, I can both be and do. This Devotional is the outgrowth of God's indwelling Spirit in me. So writing for me is not just what I do, rather it is who I am in Christ Jesus.

All seven volumes of My Little Devotional Books are designed with you the reader in mind. Each book is laid out by weeks as opposed to the traditional daily formats. If you have a small group you meet with weekly this format could work well as an icebreaker to open up the meeting for discussions about the selected scripture text. If you can spend time to read daily that's great! But if you want to go at a slower pace and spend time with a text until you have gleaned from it everything you desire or need, that's great too. The busy mother or caregiver of others can spend precious moments with God through various selected scriptures and find nourishment for her soul. The stressed father, the maxed out student, the perplexed teen, and busy musician can all feast at God's table in the other six volumes. The bonus section in this particular volume is added because of the import of the information specifically for women. It contains materials and information designed to not only nurture women, but seeks to also restore the Queen-ship God intended for every woman to enjoy...

Week One: The Black Hole of Grief

BIBLICAL REFERENCE

NO.1   Isaiah 53:4-5 (NASB)

"Surely our grief's He Himself bore, and our sorrows He carried; yet we ourselves esteemed Him stricken, smitten of God, and afflicted. But He was pierced through for our transgressions, He was crushed for our iniquities; the chastening of our well-being fell upon Him, and by His stripes we are healed."

STORY

A true close friend of mine was going through a very difficult time in her life and needed my support. I considered my friend to be a strong woman spiritually. She to me was a very capable Intercessor, and she was a woman of great faith. But I also realized that she is much like all of us who would live Godly, persecution will come our way. And no matter how strong we are in our faith in God, we are still human. This is especially important for those of us who are set apart for ministry to remember.

I felt honored that she felt close enough to me to ask my support. I was also humbled by it as well. Realizing my own inadequacies I immediately sought God for guidance on how to be of help to my friend. Through the guidance of God's Holy Spirit I was able to help my friend in her time of need. God revealed to me that my friend was grieving. Utilizing my skills as a Chaplain and partnering with the Holy Spirit I gently guided my friend through the grief process.

LESSON

No matter how strong we think we are in our Christian walk, we will all experience some type of grief. And it comes at the most vulnerable times in our lives. While books have been written about grief and we can rely on God, there is never a time when we are really prepared for it.

God used me to be a struggle buddy for my friend. I was happy to be there for her in her grief, but while helping her, it opened up some of my own "Unresolved" issues at the same time. So at times I was overwhelmed. I had to learn on the spot very often to determine what was my stuff, and what was her stuff, and then to separate the two.

In order to be there for my friend, I did not have to re-invent the box, but I needed to step outside the box. The funny thing about grief is that all grief has some of the same stuff going on, but every grief experience is different.

TESTIMONY

In my own personal experiences with grief I kept trying to be this strong Christian, and an invincible wall of strength. I went through much of my life suppressing losses and hurtful things that happened to me personally. One day I was almost on the verge of a complete breakdown. That is when I realized that I was stuck in my own black hole of grief and I couldn't get out. I was like Marvin Sapp, I never would have made it without God' grace and mercy, and I would have lost my mind.

Not only did I get the strength I needed from God, I went for the first tine to get help from a trained mental health professional. That may not be for you in managing your grief, but that is how God was leading me. Just know that sometimes God uses people to bring about our healing too.

Also remember this, the best efforts of man and modern science can only treat the symptoms of grief. God has the only cure! His power alone heals us. The scripture text tells us that by Jesus' stripes we are healed. God is the expert of grief and loss. Jesus absorbs our grief and sorrow and replaces it with the oil of joy.

PRAYER

My friend, why not take God at His word today. Give Him all of your grief and sorrows. If that is your desire pray this prayer.

Dear God of heaven, I am hurting because of the grief I am experiencing right now in my life. I surrender all of my grief and my life to You. I refuse to let Satan get a foothold on my emotions. God I desire to be healed and restored by You. I am taking You at Your word in, Isaiah 53:4-5, which tells me that by Jesus' stripes, I am healed. In Jesus' name I pray-

Amen

Week Two: Seeking God's Comfort

BIBLICAL REFERENCE
NO. 2. II Corinthians 1: 3-4 (NASB)

"Blessed be the God and Father of our Lord Jesus Christ, the Father of mercies and God of all comfort, who comforts us in all our affliction so that we will be able to comfort those who are in any affliction with the comfort with which we ourselves are comforted by God."

STORY

That word "comfort" is found within the word "comfortable". But the word "comfortable", is a horse of a different color, so to speak. The dictionary meaning for the word "comfort" is an action verb. It means to soothe or console. The word "comfortable" is an adjective. It means to be contented or at ease. It also means adequate or sufficient. If you are an English teacher you may correct me if I am wrong. I am merely trying to make a point.

The weird thing about these two meanings is that it is difficult to be comfortable when you are trying to comfort someone. So much for the, English language, "Word Study". An individual who tries to comfort another individual actually moves out of their comfort zone in order to comfort. A person can't really comfort unless they have experienced what it's like to be uncomfortable. If I don't know what it feels like to be disappointed, I won't really understand why people who are disappointed are sad. I have been disappointed many times. I know what that feels like. I have also experienced what it feels like to be rejected, and abused. It doesn't feel good. I also know what it feels like to lose a loved one.

LESSON

For me that is one of the most painful experiences ever! When someone or something you love dies the loss is experienced by all those who knew that loved one. But if you don't really know the person who died or weren't attached to the thing that died the loss is not really felt that much.

In those instances it is difficult to know how to comfort. In other words you can't comfort where you don't itch. Grief is not merely a surface ailment. Grief runs deep down on the inside, where human hands cannot reach. That's where God comes in. Only God can scratch where we don't itch. God still uses us however to offer our sympathy and support to hurting people.

When we have gone through similar experiences like those we try to comfort, we can also empathize. It doesn't take great intellect, or the brain of a rocket scientist to provide support and comfort. It does require a heart filled with love and kindness. In fact it's as simple as being available to God, and God does it through us!

TESTIMONY

God works in us through the mighty power of His Holy Spirit. So we need to stay in touch with God through prayer. We need to spend time with Him as we go through our day. When we pray for others, we get a blessing also. Something we can ask God in behalf of those, who may be hurting, is for them to give their hearts and their hurts to God.

Ask God to reveal to you how to pray for them and ways in which you can assist them. Sometimes God will use us to be the answer to our prayers for others. But in every situation we must trust God to do the very best. God is after all, the God of all comfort! If you know of someone who is hurting today, why not pray this simple prayer:

PRAYER

Dear God of heaven, your word says in, (II Corinthians 1:3-4) that you are the God of all comfort. You have been my source of comfort in my times of great need. I have experienced your awesome power, and I know what you can and will do. Use me to bring comfort and support to others. Show me how to pray for them, and answer according to your will. In the name of Jesus,

Amen.

Week Three: Angels Watching Over Me

BIBICAL REFERENCE

NO. 3. Psalms 91:11 (NASB)

"For He will command His Angels concerning you, to guard you in all your ways."

STORY

I love angels! The good angels are the ones I love of course. I was browsing the shelves of a local Christian book store, searching for books on angels. I found this amazing book about angels titled, "The Truth about Angels", by E. G. White. I would gladly recommend this book to anyone wanting to know more about angels like I did.

This book is for skeptics as well, who, may not even believe angels exist. The book forwards the idea that angels actually existed prior to the creation of mankind. The book talks about there being angels in heaven assigned to carry little children that died while living on earth to their mother's arms in heaven. How comforting is that thought to those who have lost children here on this earth!

LESSON

Believe it or not there are a great number of people who like me, believe that angels do exist. There are lots of stories of people who have been visited by angels. My son William was sure he had an encounter with an angel when he was a small child. He related to me that he and his brothers were walking home from the store one day. At the time he didn't know there was a gang of boys hiding just ahead of them, planning to jump them. He recalled a huge man appearing in front of him and writing the word run in bold red letters in the sky. He immediately told his brothers to run! They ran past the gang and were chased by them. Because the angel had warned my son, they had a big head start and the gang couldn't catch up with them. My sons got home safely and were unharmed. The angel's warning was very timely.

TESTIMONY

I believe my guardian angel protected me from danger too one day. I had begun a new temporary job assignment in downtown Denver Colorado USA. It was one early fall morning in 1997. It was very early in the morning before the sun came up and I was walking briskly to get to the office.

That morning I got off the bus closer to the building where I worked because I was running a little late. Although that route was closer, it meant I would have to take a narrow secluded street in order to get there. I felt a little uneasy as I was walking, so the words to a Christian song came to my mind and I began to sing it. You won't believe this, but the song was about angels!

As I walked, I sang the words to the song over and over, "All night all day angels watching over me my Lord, all night, all day angels watching over me." As I was singing I saw out of my peripheral vision to my left a suspicious looking man. He was blasting obscenities and stumbling forward as he walked. At first he was on the opposite side of the street, but I noticed him coming over towards me. A chill came over me and I began to walk faster.

I kept singing, and I began to sing louder. I could sense that the man was trying to catch up to me. Suddenly a relieved feeling started to rise up in me. I turned around to see what was happening. The man had stopped walking towards me as though someone was in front of him blocking him. I really believe my guarding angel and perhaps other angels had gathered around me to protect me.

PRAYER

The Holy Bible has many stories in it that tell of angels that do God's biddings, and angel visitations. It also talks about fallen angels. Fallen angels are evil angels. They exist because of sin. My friend what do you believe about angels? If you want to know the truth about angels, why not pray to God to guide you?

Dear God of heaven, I believe You want me to know the truth about angels. Please open my mind to what You would have me know about them. Thank you for hearing my prayer. In the name of Jesus I pray- Amen

Week Four: A Shelter in the Time of Trouble

BIBICAL REFERENCE
NO. 4. Psalms 27:5 (NIV)

"For in the Day of Trouble He will keep me safe in His dwelling; He will hide me in the shelter of His tabernacle and set me high upon a rock."

STORY

I recall the time when trouble was my bed-fellow so to speak. I was a student in University in Michigan. I had to work part-time to make ends meet. I was not only working toward a degree, I had to provide for myself and three sons who lived with me at the time. So in the evening after I finished my classes for the day, I went to work at a Women's Shelter.

My shift began around 6:P.M. four days a week. The shelter was situated in a small rural community nestled between lots of foliage and tall trees. My shift ended around midnight. That meant I had to drive the dark, dangerous winding roads from the shelter to get back to my home in Berrien Springs, Michigan. I always became very troubled in my spirit when it was time to make that drive home after work.

Sometimes I was the only car on that dark stretch home for miles and miles. I was really uneasy when a truck or car would suddenly appear in my rear-view mirror with their bright light beams shining into my car. My fear would intensify at those times and I would speed up to get as far away from them as possible. I felt a little better on nights when the moonlight offered some lighting on those dark stretches of road. I also felt a sense of relief when I reached near where I lived. At least there were street lights in the areas near my home. However, It wasn't until I felt the shelter of my home that I was at peace.

LESSON

I'm sometimes mindful of those songs we sing that speak to a familiar dilemma we know as "trouble". One of those songs goes something like this, "Trouble in my way, I have to cry sometimes." Have you ever experienced trouble? If you haven't, just you live on long enough, and trouble will come knocking on your door.

We may be up today, but tomorrow we may be down. One thing that I know that makes me glad is this. Trouble don't last always. My trouble may be different form yours, but we all have similar things that trouble us. Trouble may mean the inability to meet our monthly mortgage payments. It could be facing foreclosure. Maybe it is more up close and personal, your marriage is in shambles. Maybe your stocks took a tremendous plunge or your "401K" disappeared because of a catastrophic illness the insurance did not cover.

For the wealthy it might mean you had to file bankruptcy for the first time in your life and you are suddenly poor. Whatever you call trouble, I want you to know there is a way out. I call Him Jesus. He declares in His Word that He is the way, the truth, and the Light.

I know that God will make a way somehow. The text in Psalms 27:5 tells us that God will keep us safe in His shelter.

TESTIMONY

It's like that with my experience with God. He provides shelter from the troubles and storms in my life. God offers each of us that same shelter in His dwelling place. To get to it we only need to open our heart and invite him into our life to be our God.

It's funny, but when we are in God's shelter nothing can harm us and we can always find the peace we need. God does not merely hide us from harm, He also elevates our minds. He places us high upon a firm foundation. That rock is Christ Jesus! How wonderful is that! Why not try God's shelter from your troubles and storms. If that is your desire pray this prayer.

PRAYER

Dear God of heaven, send forth Your light to brighten my little corner of this dark world. Come into my heart and hide me in the shelter of Your loving arms. Guide me safely to your dwelling. In the name of Jesus I pray- Amen

Week Five: God the Marriage Expert

BIBICAL REFERENCE

NO. 5. Genesis 2:18

"The Lord said, it is not good for man to be alone. I will make a helper suitable for him."

STORY

I have been married twice. I am not proud of that fact. In fact I actually took my marriage vows seriously both times. It just so happened that I married the wrong men. How I managed to do that twice I'm not sure.

Anyway I was around thirty something and in my second marriage. By then I finally began to realize married life is not a fairytale. I also came to the conclusion that I was pretty much like the woman in the poem by Langston Hughes, "Mother to Son", "Life for me ain't been no crystal stairs".

Unlike my first husband, my second husband leaned on me much too much to get the majority of his needs met. My needs didn't matter much at all to him. He bragged about being self-sufficient when it came to ironing and cooking.

That may have been true, but I couldn't tell. His demands for freshly laundered, and ironed shirts, was always more than I was able to keep up with. One day it came to a head.

He had looked into the closet for a shirt and did not find one there. He looked at me with this expression of disgust and loathing towards me. I felt the tension rise and swell up inside of me. I was almost in a rage, but I tried to not really show it, for fear of what would happen. My husband had a good side and a bad side. I had seen firsthand his bad side and I didn't intend to stir it up. Somehow I did manage to take up for myself that day. I expressed to him as calmly as possible that I was completely exhausted, and simply could no longer do or be whatever it was he expected me to do or be.

LESSON

My plate was always too full of things to do back then. I worked full-time outside of the home, did everything I could to make sure food was cooked, the house was presentable, and clothes were clean for all seven of us in the household, plus my own stuff.

To make things worse, I was sick most of the time with a Kidney disease called "Polycystic Kidney Disease". There were days I could barely manage to get out of bed, but I made myself keep on going. I was hospitalized more than once with complications from the Illness in my body.

I wanted to be all I could be for everyone I loved then, but I could only do so much. I sensed that I was not the helper that God intended for my husband, and even more so not at all suitable for him. I went into periods of depression and experienced a lot of unhealthy mood swings while I was in that marriage.

I tried to keep it going in spite of all the signs that it was not working. Although I was a faithful wife, my husband was not faithful to me. That only added to my depression and mood swings. Finally we separated and many years went by. We never reconciled the wrongs in our marriage.

Eventually we divorced. After the divorce, I made a vow that I would never marry again. I felt that I was a complete failure. A Christian counselor pointed out to me one day that I was being unfair to God with that kind of ultimatum. He explained to me that God may have the right man for me to be my husband, but if I have my mind made up to never marry again, I will never know it. So I recanted my position on marriage after that.

TESTIMONY

God really is the expert when it comes to marriage. Man can only hope for the best outcome in a marriage when, God does not do the matching. The scripture text tells us that God will bring together a helper for the man, who will be suitable for him. That means the guesswork is not there.

So when we ask God for a good husband, He will match us with someone that we can please. When we pray to God for Him to give us a husband, we can be confident that God will give to us His very best! What do you want God to do in regard to marriage for you? No relationship is too difficult for God. Do you want to have the marriage that God designed? Why not pray to God for it.

PRAYER

I have included a bonus section that addresses the matter of marriage and male/female relationships in the back section of this book. Among the materials available in it is a suggested "Marriage Prayer" for your use. Whatever your situation might be, my prayer for you is that God will bless you with the desires of your heart.

Week Six: The Family of God

BIBLICAL REFERENCE

NO. 6. Mark 3:35 (NIV)

"Whoever does God's will is my brother and sister and mother."

STORY

Family seems to be the backbone of most mainstream societies. While this is true the family dynamics have changed and evolved drastically. What constitutes a family in America and other countries around the world is as varied and different as cultures allows. It has been suggested by some who study people and cultures, that the barometer of a society can best be understood by the way in which it views the women in that society.

The origin of family can be dated as far back as the Biblical account of Adam and Eve. The first family consisted of a father, mother, and children. A marriage consisted of one man and one woman. That changed in time to allow a man to have multiple wives. The idea of a woman having multiple husbands was not acceptable. The concept of the extended- family, and blended-family are not unique to our day and time. The one parent family is very common today.

Family can take on a different nature depending on the function of a family. For example there is the church family; the crime families; families that are made up of blood relatives and those in which the person is considered a part of the family by association.

When I was matriculating through University I acquired lots of nieces and nephews by association. My friends who had children were instructed to call me aunt Lolita. I did the same with my children. So my sons had many aunts and uncles as a result.

LESSON

Jesus was part of a traditional family growing up, but it was also possibly a blended family because Joseph had been married prior to his marriage to Mary the mother of Jesus. Now Jesus also had a different idea about what he considered to be His family. You may even know the story found in Mark chapter three. It happened something like this.

One day Jesus entered a house. While he was inside the crowd was so great his family became concerned for His safety, and for His reputation. They thought that Jesus must have lost His mind to be surrounded by such a great throng of people He didn't know. Nothing could have been farther from the truth. The Women's Bible Commentary Expanded Edition, by Carol A. Newsom and Sharon H. Ridge offers this spin on the event and an interesting narrative.

They suggest that the Bible account sheds a possible negative portrayal of Jesus' family on this particular day. Let's explore the meaning of "family" in the Greek language. It meaning is actually literal, "Those near Him". They go on to suggest that His family considered Jesus to be insane! They explain that while it was only Jesus' family who called Him into question in the scriptures, some of His disciples may have been with the family when they were seeking Jesus to inquire of His actions as well.

Additionally the authors forward the idea that on this particular occasion the crowd was so large that it hindered Jesus from taking care of His personal needs. For example He was prevented from eating. His family saw this as unacceptable behavior. They felt that Jesus was out of control. Some of the crowd felt that perhaps Jesus might even be demon possessed.

No matter what the opinions were about Jesus, His accusers were rebuked by Him. Newsom and Ridge suggest that the real problem Jesus had with His family and others accusing Him, was, that they failed to view Jesus as "The Christ"! They held to their narrow world view of Jesus. So His neighbors and kin misinterpreted Jesus' actions through conventional social relational norms. They were oblivious to the "new family" Jesus is establishing. Jesus idea of "family" is those who do God's will.

TESTIMONY

I grew up in a traditional family structure. I had a mother, a father, and siblings. But I also had two older sisters that had a different father but the same mother as me. They were born to a different marriage and I did not grow up a part of that household.

My mother married as a teenager and gave birth to my two sisters. There was a twenty year time span between my oldest brother and my two sisters. I was also a part of an extended family which included grandparents etc... I never knew what it was like to not be a part of a family. In that sense I feel blessed. There are orphans in our society that have no family. That is very sad.

I have a lot of respect for those who adopt children. If you are part of a loving family never take that for granted. Everyone wants and deserves to be loved.

PRAYER

What is your idea of family? No matter what that looks like, Jesus is inviting you to become a part of His "new family" today. You can become a part of the family of God by praying this simple prayer:

Dear God of heaven, teach me to do "Your" will. Make the path to obedience to You clear, and plain before me. Lord Jesus in whom the family of earth, and the family of heaven are made one; I desire to become born again into "Your" family. I pray this prayer in the name of Jesus, and to "Your" glory dear God-

Amen

Week Seven: A Victorious Life

BIBLICAL REFERENCE

NO. 7. Psalms 108:13

"With God we will gain the victory, and He will trample down our enemies"

STORY

I had the pleasure of delivering a sermon about "Victory" to a group of Asian students in South Korea some years ago. I was a Missionary working as an English teacher at the Korean SDA English Institute at the time. In my sermon I presented "victory" in terms of success in life. I used racing as an example of how to achieve success.

My anchor text was from (1Corinthians 9:24 NIV), *"Do you not know that in a race all the runners run, but only one gets the prize? Run in such a way as to get the prize."* In other words run to not merely be in the race, but to also gain the prize. Victory is the prize for those who do battle with God, but the finish or the prize is not realized until the enemy is trampled down by God! Every Christian who loves God has an enemy. That enemy is Satan.

We can't fight the enemy Satan in our strength alone. Satan is too strong for us, but not for God to defeat. You may not be a Christian. The enemy is still Satan. Satan does not care if you are a Christian. He will take anyone down he can. His goal is to kill you and destroy any chance you might have to receive the gift of eternal life. The gift of eternal life is free. We can't buy it nor earn it; it is absolutely free. The only way we can have this free gift is through Jesus Christ, the Son of God.

LESSON

Let's go back to the "race". The Bible has something else to say about the "race" that is worth examining. Ecclesiastes 9:24 says, *"I have seen something else under the sun; The race is not to the swift...."* For every Christian the "race" can be regarded as the path of life that we take.

The winner is not the one who runs the fastest, but the one who finishes or endures to the end. The fastest runner might run ahead of God instead of following God. The fastest runner will often forget to stop and smell the roses God has placed strategically along the path. They may miss the important sign-post that offer them sound instruction and direction.

They won't stop long enough to drink from the river of life. They will pass up wisdom, sound judgment, and discernment. The path of life for the Christian runner will be rocky sometimes, but God will make the path doable by subduing our enemy under our feet. If we endure to the end God has for us a crown of life!

(James 1:12 NIV) says, *"Blessed is the man who perseveres under the trial, because he has stood the test, he will receive the crown of life that God has promised to those who love Him"*. What Christian would not want to finish the race?

Some people get success and living a victorious life mixed up. Beth Moore author of the book "Praying God's Word" gives an interesting take on this matter. She shares her life experience this way, "I had lived successfully for years…but not victoriously. Oh, how wise we are to understand the mammoth difference." She goes on to explain that "successfully" can describe how we handle relatively manageable challenges.

Anyone can do the relatively manageable. Victoriously according to Beth Moore, describes how we live as over-comers in the midst of Goliath oppositions. That kind of opposition is orchestrated by our enemy Satan and can only be destroyed by the power of God. How are you living your life today? Maybe things for you are manageable, but your want more out of life.

TESTIMONY

This is a silly question for you. Do you have enemies? I believe we all have at least one enemy. One school of thought regarding enemies is this, "If you are not for me, then you are against me". Now we don't necessarily have to even know our enemy. But our enemy certainly exist. Someone may even consider us to be their enemy.

Enemies come in all sizes and all sorts of packaging. Some are of the notion that it's best to keep our friends close to us, and our enemies even closer. Actually that makes a lot of sense. Knowing who your enemy is and where they are is a true advantage. Maybe this discussion seems farfetched and not relevant.   But wait!

Before you put this book down; just bear with me for a little while longer. Let's pretend you do have at least one enemy. While I have your attention; let's continue. I'm going to switch lanes now and talk about "victory". Victory can be bitter-sweet at times.

In victory's quake comes both ecstasy and agony. In the text for this week, the word "with" implies that we have a part in the battle. With God we are assured of victory. With God there is not only an expected outcome for us, our enemy will be trampled down!

PRAYER

Why not do battle with your enemy Satan with God as your strength? Aren't you tired of doing things on your own, and tired of being sick and tired? If you want to live a victorious life, pray this prayer:

Dear God of heaven, I have been fighting my battles in my own strength. I gain some ground, but my enemy is too strong for me. I want to live a victorious life from now on. Please come into my life and heart and fill me with Your Holy Spirit.

I want to be an over-comer and wear a crown of life when I come to the end of my life here on this earth. I want to receive the free gift of eternal life right now by inviting Jesus to be my personal Savior. Thank You for giving me everything I have asked for. I pray this prayer in the name of Jesus-

Amen

Bonus Section

This section is going to take you to places that you thought only you have been. The contents are not the average traditional materials you may have read in an inspirational book for or about women. I had actually completed the Bonus Section of My Little Devotional Book Vol. III, and God directed me to pick up a book I have had in my personal library for some time, (The Power of Being A Real Woman, by Jennifer Keitt).

I had leafed through it on one or more occasions, but never really picked it up to actually read it thoroughly. You may have that kind of book in your possession too. But I believe that God directed me to this book because of the subject matter that will be presented in the Bonus Section of My Little Devotional Book Vol. III, and the import it holds for the women who are often forgotten about or have been spurned and abused.

Those of us women who are survivors of abuse still need this information as well. Along with my book I would recommend to every woman to make Jennifer Keitt's book, and Gayle Taylor's "Encompassing" materials that are included in my book a "must have" part of your personal library.

Chapter seven of Keitt's book (Today's Christian Woman and Sex-Healing for Our Souls) is quite explicit and candid! Keitt says, "Sex is not a topic discussed openly, thoroughly, and thoughtfully, like we're so in need of as women..." She goes on to explain that God is fully aware of what we as women are in need of in regard to our sexuality. She forwards the idea that God is willing and ready to reconcile us back to Himself in the area of our female sexuality. Keitt suggest that God also knows that we His daughters are not complete, victorious, whole sexual beings.

She further suggest that we are actually incompetent, hurt, abused, trapped, frustrated and discouraged when it comes to the subject of our sexuality, sex in our marriages, and sexual feelings we have in our singleness. Keitt qualifies her assertions by stating that "Jesus" is the answer. Keitt's book deals with those hard topics like Incest; Molestation; Rape; Adultery; Pornography; Sodomy; Fornication; Homosexuality; Affairs; Flirting; Masturbation; Cruelty; Abuse, and Bareness.

What Keitt discusses in her book is on point with what this Bonus Section is all about. I agree with much of what Keitt says in her book, especially in regard to how God thinks about women and our sexuality. Get ready to dismiss any myths or misconceptions you might have about your sexuality. God wants us to be whole as well as informed in this area of our womanhood.

This Bonus Section is also about the "new thing" God is doing in the earth with those who hear and are willing to answer the clarion call of God. The 21st century woman of God is fashioned according to Jeremiah 31:22 (NASB), "... *For the Lord has created a new thing in the earth. A woman will encompass a man."* Women who desire to know about "Encompassing", or are already enlightened in regard to "Encompassing", can benefit greatly from the materials in this bonus section.

According to the Women's Bible Commentary Expanded Edition, God's promise is actually translated from the original language as a literal action. A woman is to actually encompass a man. I think that can best be understood in terms of the woman acting in behalf of the man as his protector.

Sense the woman is considered to be the weaker vessel protection would most likely come by way of providing a prayer covering. In either sense this could be considered as a new role for women. Sense God is calling forth this act and putting His stamp of approval upon it, this is a God idea. Encompassing should therefore be something women should readily seek to do!

I can think of several ways in which women might pray for their men. One area that is under attack by Satan frequently regarding our men is in relationships. Another critical area is their sexuality. You will find that every area of a man's life and well-being could benefit significantly from an encompassing woman's protection.

Much of the materials in the bonus section has been provided courtesy of Gayle Taylor founder of "New Thing Sisters" and "Ewe-Glow, Girl! Ewe Two" Ministries. Gayle is a powerful woman of God and her teachings on "Encompassing" have proved to be invaluable to me as a mother of four sons and a minister of God.

I have been blessed to discover how it pays to pray to God for A God- sent husband using Gayle's materials, and to wait on God for the right one suited just for me. When I discovered that my adult first born son was suffering under the bondage of an addiction, I was able to use some of Gayle's encompassing instructional materials to encompass him, and pray for his deliverance.

Gayle believes that as encompassing women we can exact victory and deliverance for our men that would not be evident without our prayers to God in their behalf. There are several suggested prayers provided in the Bonus Section that are sure to be helpful to you as you endeavor to encompass the men in your life.

My earnest prayer for you is that encompassing will be something that you will embrace for yourself and that great and mighty and wonderful blessings are manifested in your life. May God be glorified as you seek to become all that God desires for you to be. May your Queen-ship be restored a thousand times over and the men in your life be truly blessed to receive love from you fit for a King.

Queen-Ship Restored: Mindset of Love Fit For a King

What About Me?? Prayers

Suggested Prayers for The Jeremiah 31:22 Woman

<u>What I need /Want prayers</u>: This prayer considers the parts of our love for our men that meets their sexual needs and for intimacy. Remember that sex should be restricted to married couples only!

1. Most Holy Creator, You made my man's body. You designed it so that his sexual fluids build up every seventy-two hours. The pressure that this puts upon him calls for me to be sensitive to and mindful of his needs. Enable me to be comfortable with sexual contact with my man. Place within me creativity and equip me with delightful techniques that will tantalize him and bring optimum pleasure. May we both truly enjoy the experience. Remove from within me everything that would hinder me from being ready to fulfill this part of our marriage. May Your Word dear God according to Proverbs 31:22a (NIV) *"She makes coverings for her bed;"* be honored in this prayer.

What I need /Want prayers: This prayer puts us as women into the habit of attending to the area in which our men are hit the hardest; the area of "seduction"!

2. Eternal God of heaven, You can see all of the tricks, traps and snares set up by others for my man. He may even be seduced by men who desire or enjoy same sex. My man needs protection from any attack on his sexuality. I ask your divine supernatural protection over my man continuously; especially in his times of weakness or vulnerability. I ask your divine covering and the blood of Jesus to be applied over his sexual nature at all times. May it be to him according to Your Word in Song of Solomon 7:10, *"I belong to my lover and his desire is for me."*

What I need/Want prayers: This prayer actually takes our mind off what we want for ourselves and helps us to really focus on his needs.

3. Greatest God over all things in the universe, grant me mental; emotional; physical and spiritual health so that I can meet all of my man's needs. I ask that You remove all things from my character and life that would prevent me from being at my optimized best at all times. Bless me with a personality that brings into our space laughter, fun, and variety. Adorn me with colors that attract and soothe him. Reveal his unspoken needs to me so that I

can readily respond to them. Enable me to hear from you and follow your guidance concerning his every need. Show me daily what to pray for in his behalf. Please answer this prayer according to Your Word in Psalms 139:23, 24b (NIV) that says, *"Search me oh God, test me and know my hear t; test me and know my anxious thoughts... and lead me in the way everlasting."*

Queen-Ship Restored: Relationship Love Fit For a King

The next three prayers express concerns that speak to where you as a woman or young woman might be. Some of the prayer's content is often overlooked in traditional prayers.

What I need/Want prayers: **This prayer removes any known or unknown blocks you may have that prevent you from being in a healthy relationship with a man.**

1. Dear Lord, You see my past and you know my future. I ask for total healing of all past hurts. Father You know the path that I take and my journey. Remake and reshape and fashion me free of past abuses. Heal me of what I have gone through physically, emotionally, mentally and spiritually in my life that has left me wounded. Enable me to break free of a "victim" mentality. Thank You for loving me enough to not leave me in my broken state. Please answer this prayer according to Psalms 147:3 (NASB) that says, *"He heals the broken hearted and binds up their wounds."*

What I need/Want prayers: **This prayer takes away fears of losing your man through relational conflicts. It puts to rest fears of abuse or violence if and whenever you are in disagreement with your man.**

2. Dear God in heaven, I believe that Your best for me, is a man who will communicate with me in a healthy positive manner. He will confer with me in all major important decisions. Help us both to be willing to say "I'm sorry" and mean it. Equip both of us with problem-solving skills that create a "win-win" situation for the two of us. Help us to each resolve to give 100% of ourselves to the relationship realizing that this is what God desires for us. Please answer this prayer according to Your Word in Colossians 2:2 (RSV) that says, *"That their hearts may be encouraged being knit together in love, and attaining to all riches of the full assurance of understanding, of knowledge and mystery of God, both of the Father and Christ."*

<u>What I need/Want prayers</u>: This prayer takes away negative ideas placed into our minds about men and the illegal use of male power that is socially acceptable and represented as the "status-quo".

3. Dear loving Father in heaven, I want to be the very best gift that my man can receive. Look deep inside me and reveal to me areas of rebellion and disobedience to You that will hinder what You're are trying to process in me. I am willing to surrender to you completely my sexuality dear God. Re-work in me Your optimum divine character and nature. Enable me to trust you completely and to then trust the man You have given me to love. May this prayer be answered according to Your Word in I Corinthians 1:3,7 (NIV) that says, *" Now I want you to realize*

that the head of every man is Christ, and the head of the woman is man, and the head of Christ is God… A man ought not to cover his head, since he is the image of the glory of God; but the woman is the glory of man."

Marriage Prayer
(For those contemplating marriage)

Dear Heavenly Father, Your counsel regarding marriage
Has been revealed in Your Word, by the power of Your Holy
Spirit. I desire to enter into my marital relationship with
Your full blessings.

You said in Your Word that it is not good that man should be
alone
(Gen. 2:18-24). I believe that You will join me with my heart
companion.
And that this individual would be lost without me as his wife. I
have
Been assigned by You oh God (through revealed knowledge and
the
Leading of Your Holy Spirit) to be in
Your perfect will regarding my marriage partner.
Because You oh God are doing the choosing, I believe that
He will be suitable in every detail.

Open my heart companion's eyes to see me as his wife and queen. May
He also see me as his "helpmeet" and "Queen Warrior". May he desire
To make me a permanent part of his life, by
Asking me to be his wife.

Teach me oh God how to crown him as a "King" and to affirm his
Authority over me in the marital relationship. Endow me with the grace to always respect him as such before others
Wherever I may be.

Thank You for hearing and answering my prayer.
In Jesus' name – Amen

By LS REED

About The Author

Lolita resides in Denver, Colorado. She has two adult sons Juan L. Reed and Michael K. Reed. Lolita holds several degrees and completed the required year of Clinical Pastoral education and Chaplain Residency program at Porter Hospital in Denver Colorado in 1997. She has done volunteer work as a Prison Chaplain in Alabama, and Indiana.

Lolita worked with several Women's Shelters in Michigan and held numerous leadership positions within and outside of her church denomination over the span of three decades. She shares that the most rewarding assignment for her was as a Volunteer Missionary in South Korea from February 2002 through August 2004. All of the things she has done or accomplished she attributes to the anointing of God upon her life.

If anyone knows Lolita at all they know that she is basically a people person. She loves people! What is so crazy about this fact is that she also has an introverted personality. The reason she can be an introvert and love people is but God…! It's the love and power of God that drives her to seek out people and to engage with them in a quality manner. If she could, she would love to heal everybody she met who is broken just like Jesus did.

Lolita shares that God has moved in her life, (supernaturally at times) and cleaned up her stuff. But it is that stuff she has gone through that makes it easy for her to resonate with a lot of what is going on with the myriad of women she meets. Her travels in the US and abroad afford her a wider and deeper world view from which to operate. Lolita says she gets excited when she can share her experiences with other women and we each have a mutual respect for God and each other. And that she almost always walks away from these encounters with more wisdom and a deeper understanding of who God is!

She feels that when she leaves the choices up to God and just simply makes herself available to Him, then she is led to connect with the most amazingly incredible people! Her insurance Agent is an example of one of those people. Lolita shares that she met Karen in 2006 when God blessed her to purchase a car. She didn't just sell me car insurance explains Lolita; she made me feel special as a customer. She was so kind that I even switched over my home insurance to her company.

With a good portion of the proceeds from the sell of this book, Lolita would like to set up a program that will assist "at risk" women who are willing to turn their lives around. The program would work with car dealerships to secure suitable cars for these women and provide paid-up car insurance for at least six months to give them a heads up.

Lolita relates how God worked through a fellow Seminary student when she so desperately needed a car. The student not only blessed her with a car. He paid for the car in full and gave it to her absolutely free! He also paid six months of car insurance for the car. Lolita says she didn't have to pay back one penny. She remembers that as the nicest thing anyone had ever done for her. She says she will never forget that act of kindness. Lolita plans to pay it forward by doing the same for others.

If you have purchased this book you are bringing her one step closer to making her dream a reality. May you have a hundred fold return for your kindness and your spiritual cup be overflowing with God's love. Lolita is looking forward to perhaps singing a copy of this book for you some day. If we don't meet somehow in this life, then perhaps for sure in heaven. Pray that we all will be there...

FOR MORE INFORMATION

Keitt, Jennifer, The Power Of Being A Black Woman (Today's Black Woman Corp. Pub., 2001)

Taylor, Gayle, Queen-Ship Restored: Love Fit for A King (PO Box 1122 Denver, CO., 80201)

www.ingramcontent.com/pod-product-compliance
Lightning Source LLC
Chambersburg PA
CBHW051718040426
42446CB00008B/953